Abe Lincoln Remembers

ANN TURNER

Abe Lincoln Remembers

PICTURES BY WENDELL MINOR

SCHOLASTIC INC.
New York Toronto London Auckland Sydney
Mexico City New Delhi Hong Kong Buenos Aires

When I was little,
the cabin we lived in was small
with one room and one window.
At first I thought the sky was square
like a piece of cut cloth.
I could only see two birds in the sky
and one squirrel in the tree.

When I got bigger,
Pa told me my legs were like a colt's,
and he was afraid I'd fall down,
they were so long and shanky.
Sometimes I went to school, but
I don't suppose those days would add up
to much more than a year.
I'd fold up my legs like an umbrella
and sit quiet at the back of the schoolroom,
gulping down learning like water.
But Pa wouldn't allow me much schooling,
making me chop wood, build fences,
plant corn, and drive the horses.

I did learn to read, though,
got some history and my numbers.
I'd practice them on the back
of the fire shovel,
for soot and ashes make a fine slate.
And I would do anything for a book.
I'd read any chance I got
and dreamed of freedom,
of rising like a hawk into the sky
to some fine, high place.

It was time to move on.
I left, no money in hand,
no second shirt, just a handkerchief
around a piece of corn bread.
I worked on a flatboat,
and in a general store.

When the storekeeper saw
how I towered over the others,
he bet I'd whip the best
wrestler around—Jack Armstrong.
We locked arms and bodies,
swung back and forth,
then he downed me with a leg throw
the rules did not allow.
But I shook hands with him,
and we became friends.

I knew that being tall is not enough
to make your way in this world.
I needed words for that.
When I studied to become a lawyer,
I practiced my cases out loud as I walked,
learning how to use words
like a leading rein on a colt
to take people where I wanted.
But when I ran for the legislature,
I saw it would take a deal of tugging
to persuade people that slavery was wrong.

Then I found Mary, who agreed
to be my wife.
She was bright and brave
like a flag cracking in the wind,
all color, rustle, and shine.
When I ran for the Senate, she told me,
"You will win, and someday
you will be President."
How I laughed at that!
But later, others thought the same,
and I was nominated to run for the highest office.
I talked and debated
to show people we must be one nation,
not part slave, not part free.

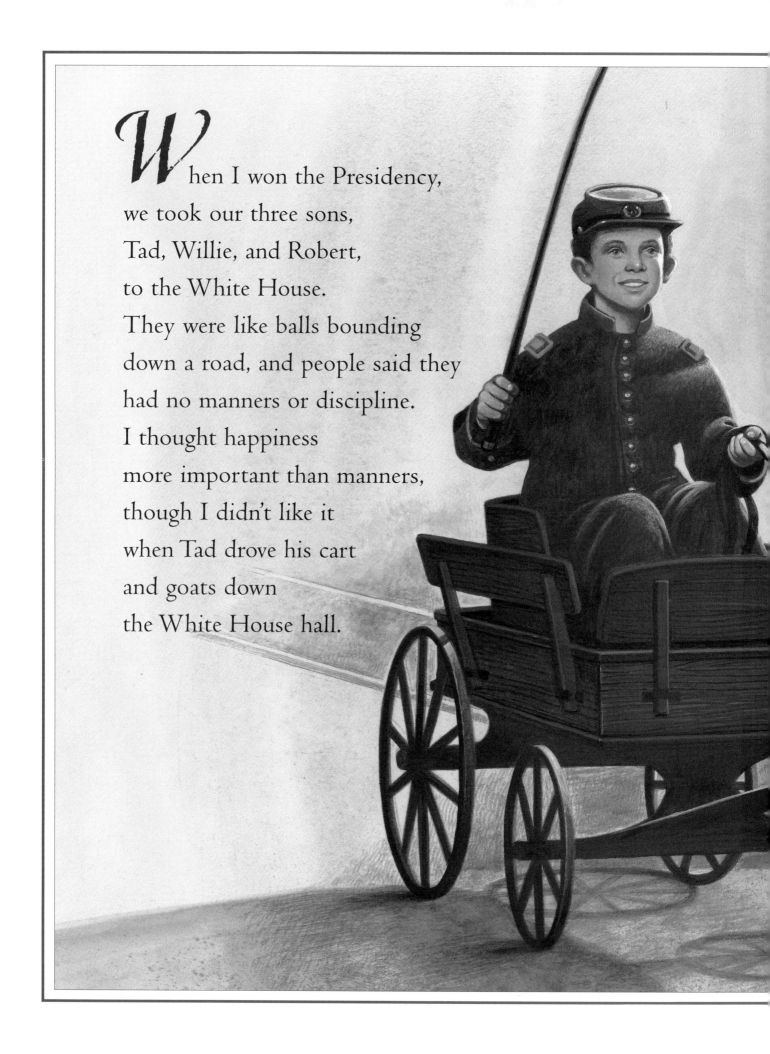

When I won the Presidency,
we took our three sons,
Tad, Willie, and Robert,
to the White House.
They were like balls bounding
down a road, and people said they
had no manners or discipline.
I thought happiness
more important than manners,
though I didn't like it
when Tad drove his cart
and goats down
the White House hall.

But we had need of happiness then:
for the great wound opened in the country
and in my chest—the war.
I tried to keep North and South together,
until it was clear that talk
could not mend this great division.
The dying grieved me so
that I had a joke book in my desk
to keep from weeping.

And I was terrified we would lose.
I could not find good generals,
and we lost as many battles as we won.
But when we won the Battle of Gettysburg,
it seemed the Union might prevail.

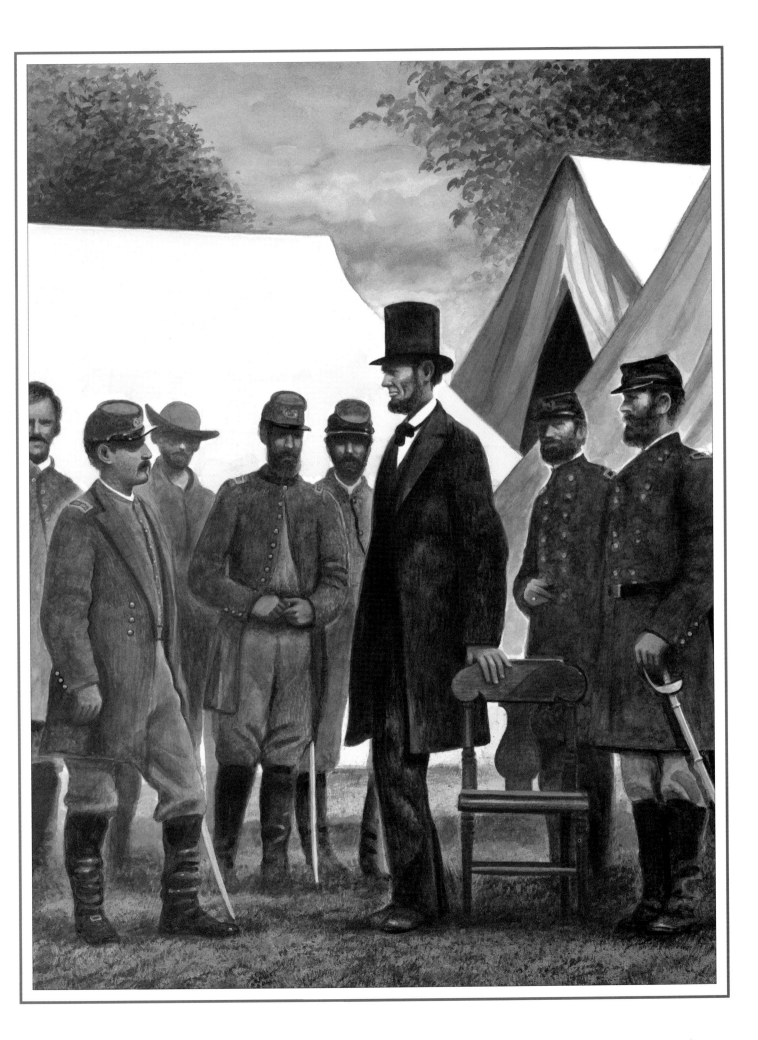

When I went and saw all those graves,
lined up like the rails I used to split,
I could hardly speak.
Words could not lead me here,
and I thought my speech a short, poor thing.
I felt in the middle of some vast tug-of-war,
until I thought my heart would break.

*F*inally our side has won, the country is not divided,
and the slaves are free.
I can be glad of that,
though when I look in the mirror,
I see how sorrow has dug lines in my cheeks.

I told Mary that tonight is a time to be happy.
As we wait to go see a play,
I think again of that little house,
the small window, the piece of sky
with two birds and one squirrel.
How much has come to pass since then.
How much there is still to be done.

A Historical Note

Shy. A dreamer. Strong. Ambitious. So tall he towered over everyone else. One of our greatest Presidents. All these descriptions applied to Abraham Lincoln.

His early years are familiar to us: born into poverty in Kentucky to a stern father and a gentle mother who died when he was still young. Some of the people who knew him then described him as "lazy," as he preferred a book to working in the field.

Leaving home at the age of twenty-two, Lincoln did many things before he settled on becoming a lawyer and going into politics. He worked in a store and as a postmaster, helped a surveyor, and ran for the state legislature in Illinois. There he announced his opposition to slavery.

Lincoln served in the United States Congress, again opposing the spread of slavery to new states. In 1860 he was chosen to be the Republican candidate and was elected President. Soon after, seven southern states declared they had left the Union.

War began, and during the early years of the Civil War, things went badly for the North. Because there were more military academies in the South, the southern forces had finer generals and more professional soldiers. Lincoln complained of his General McClellan that "he's got the slows," for he would not pursue southern troops.

Lincoln signed the Emancipation Proclamation in 1863, officially freeing all slaves. Now those freed black men could join the northern forces, which they did, helping the war effort. Finally, when Generals William Tecumseh Sherman and Ulysses S. Grant commanded the northern forces, the war turned in favor of the North.

In 1864 Lincoln was up for reelection but feared he might not win. He was not a popular president, and there was a lot of feeling against the freeing of slaves and against his conduct of the war. Lincoln knew he had to have a constitutional amendment to end slavery, to make sure the Proclamation could not be overturned. The Thirteenth Amendment to the Constitution was passed in early 1865 and ratified at the end of the year, ending slavery forever in the United States.

The war finally ended on April 9, 1865, when General Robert E. Lee, commander of the southern troops, surrendered to General Grant, commander of the Union forces. Five days later, happy that the war was over, Lincoln and his wife, Mary, went to see a play at Ford's Theater. The President's bodyguard left the Lincolns in their unlocked theater box to better see the play downstairs. While unguarded, Lincoln was shot by John Wilkes Booth and never became conscious again. Taken to a rooming house nearby, he died the following day. He was only fifty-six years old.

Abraham Lincoln was a great and inspiring president, one of the finest our country has known. His words echo down the years to us, calling to us, reminding us of what it means to lead an ethical and courageous life.

—*Ann Turner*

For my son, Ben, who is honest, like Abe
—A.T.

To my family and friends who live in THE LAND OF LINCOLN
—W.M.

AUTHOR'S NOTE

Although ABE LINCOLN REMEMBERS is based on
historical facts, it is a work of fiction. As such, this book is
intended to explore how Lincoln might have thought and felt
about the events that shaped him into one
of our greatest presidents. For the sake of the poetic
narrative, some events have been compressed. This book should
not be read as a biography but rather as an
imaginative exploration of the side of history that the facts
cannot always give us.

ISBN 0-439-33292-3

Text copyright © 2001 by Ann Turner.
Illustrations copyright © 2001 by Wendell Minor.
All rights reserved. Published by Scholastic Inc., 555 Broadway, New York, NY 10012,
by arrangement with HarperCollins Publishers.
SCHOLASTIC and associated logos are trademarks and/or registered trademarks of Scholastic Inc.

12 11 10 9 8 7 6 5 4 3 2   2 3 4 5 6 7/0

Printed in the U.S.A.   24

First Scholastic printing, January 2002

Text is set in 20-point Centaur with Ovidius light initial caps.
Book designed by Wendell Minor